The Men Who Made the Constitution

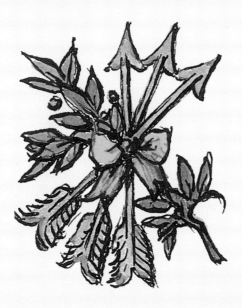

A BICENTENNIAL PORTFOLIO

In the summer of 1787, Philadelphia was the most populous American city, a bustling seaport and market town and the new nation's cultural capital. America's first permanent theater, first museum, first sectarian university, first magazine and first daily newspaper originated here. Most of the delegates who spent that hot summer in Philadelphia were lawyers, merchants and planters in their thirties and forties, men who came of age politically during the Revolution. The few older men among them, like George Washington and Benjamin Franklin, were already revered as Founding Fathers. The following pages show portraits of some of the delegates who took a prominent role in the debates and glimpses of Philadelphia about the time of the Convention.

The Constitutional Convention held its meetings at Philadelphia's State House, seen here from the northwest in a Charles Willson Peale illustration of 1778. The steeple shown in this picture deteriorated and was dismantled a few years before the Convention. In this building the Declaration of Independence was signed and George Washington was given command of the Continental Army. (Courtesy, Library of Congress)

Scenes of Philadelphia: The home of delegate Robert Morris, considered the richest man in Philadelphia, where General Washington stayed as Morris' guest during the summer of the Convention (top left, Courtesy, The Historical Society of Pennsylvania); the State House Garden (second from top left), within shouting distance of the Walnut Street Prison (below), where inmates cried out to delegates on their way to sessions (both pictures, Courtesy, Rare Book Department, Free Library of Philadelphia); Chestnut Street in downtown Philadelphia (bottom, Courtesy, Rare Book Department, Free Library of Philadelphia); the market district along High Street, where Franklin lived as a young man (top right, Courtesy, The Historical Society of Pennsylvania); Philadelphia, a bustling eighteenth-century seaport (bottom right, Courtesy, The Historical Society of Pennsylvania)

MONDAY, MAY 14TH, 1787,

Was the day fixed for the meeting of the Deputies in Convention, for revising the federal system of government. On that day a small number only had assembled. Seven States were not convened till,

FRIDAY, MAY 25TH.

When the following members appeared:
From

MASSACHUSETTS,	Rufus King.
NEW YORK,	Robert Yates, and
	Alexander Hamilton.
NEW JERSEY,	David Brearly,
	William Churchill Houston, and
	William Patterson.
PENNSYLVANIA,	Robert Morris,
	Thomas Fitzsimons,
	James Wilson, and
	Gouverneur Morris.
DELAWARE,	George Read,
	Richard Basset, and
	Jacob Broom.
VIRGINIA,	George Washington,
	Edmund Randolph,
	John Blair,
	James Madison,
	George Mason,
	George Wythe, and
	James McClurg.
NORTH CAROLINA,	Alexander Martin,
	William Richardson Davie,
	Richard Dobbs Spaight, and
	Hugh Williamson.
SOUTH CAROLINA,	John Rutledge,
	Charles Cotesworth Pinckney,
	Charles Pinckney, and
	Pierce Butler.
GEORGIA,	William Few.

Mr. ROBERT MORRIS informed the members assembled, that, by the instruction and in behalf of the deputation of Pennsylvania, he proposed GEORGE WASHINGTON, Esquire, late Commander-in-Chief, for President of the Convention. Mr. JOHN RUTLEDGE seconded the motion, expressing his confidence that the choice would be unanimous; and observing, that the presence of General WASHINGTON forbade any observations on the occasion which might otherwise be proper.

General WASHINGTON was accordingly unanimously elected by ballot, and conducted to the Chair by Mr. R. MORRIS and Mr. RUTLEDGE; from which, in a very emphatic manner, he thanked the Convention for the honor they had conferred on him; reminded them of the novelty of the scene of business in which he was to act, lamented his want of better qualifications, and claimed the indulgence of the House towards the involuntary errors which his inexperience might occasion.

George Washington at the time of the Convention (Portrait by Charles Willson Peale/Courtesy, The Pennsylvania Academy of the Fine Arts)

James Madison, who was instrumental in assembling the Constitutional Convention, establishing its agenda, and winning public approval of the final document, is also our best source for what went on in the daily sessions. His journal, written in his own shorthand during the debates and partially expanded afterward, was found among his posthumous papers and published in 1840. Except where noted, quotations in this portfolio are taken from Madison's Journal. (Portrait by Charles Willson Peale/Courtesy, The Thomas Gilcrease Institute of American History and Art, Tulsa, Oklahoma)

Alexander Hamilton, one of the three delegates from New York, surprised and shocked his colleagues with his recommendations for an all-powerful central government, his admiration for the British system of government, and his belief in a ruling aristocracy: "Let one branch of the Legislature hold their places for life, or at least during good behaviour. Let the Executive, also, be for life....The English model was the only good one on this subject." (Portrait by John Trumbull/Courtesy, Yale University Art Gallery, Trumbull Collection)

George Mason of Virginia argued for popular participation in government: "Mr. Mason argued strongly for an election of the larger branch by the people. It was to be the grand depository of the democratic principle of government. It was, so to speak, to be our House of Commons." As the Convention drew to a close without providing for civil liberties, Mason argued for a Bill of Rights and for a second convention to be held after hearing the opinions of the people: "This Constitution had been formed without the knowledge or idea of the people....It was improper to say to the people, take this or nothing." (D. W. Boudet, after a lost portrait by John Hesselius/Courtesy, Virginia Museum of Fine Arts, Richmond)

Edmund Randolph of Virginia, a protégé of Madison, introduced the Virginia Plan as an agenda and argued against a strong central government and powerful chief executive, even to the point of proposing a multiple presidency: "He could not see why the great requisites of the executive department...could not be found in three men as well as in one man. The Executive ought to be independent. It ought, therefore, in order to support its independence, to consist of more than one." At the end Randolph withheld his signature from the Constitution: "Was he to promote the establishment of a plan, which he verily believed would end in tyranny?" (Portrait by Flavius J. Fisher/Courtesy, Virginia State Library)

Roger Sherman of Connecticut found a way out of the disputes over how the states should be represented in the Congress: "Mr. Sherman proposed, that the proportion of suffrage in the first branch should be according to the respective numbers of free inhabitants; and that in the second branch, or Senate, each State should have one vote and no more." (Portrait by Ralph Earl/Courtesy, Yale University Art Gallery)

Elbridge Gerry of Massachusetts was a gadfly at the convention, objecting to both strong central authority and a popular voice in government: "Mr. Gerry did not like the election by the people....The evils we experience flow from the excess of democracy." (Courtesy, Culver Pictures)

Gouverneur Morris of Pennsylvania (sitting, in the portrait at left), who worked on the final draft and gave the Constitution much of its literary elegance, argued for putting aside the differences that had broken out during the debates: "The moment this plan goes forth, all other considerations will be laid aside, and the great question will be, shall there be a National Government, or not? and this must take place, or a general anarchy will be the alternative."

Robert Morris of Pennsylvania, financier of the Revolution, proposed General Washington as president of the convention (Portrait by Charles Willson Peale/Courtesy, The Pennsylvania Academy of the Fine Arts)

"Whilst the last members were signing, Doctor Franklin looking towards the President's chair, at the back of which a rising sun happened to be painted, observed to a few members near him, that painters had found it difficult to distinguish in their art, a rising, from a setting sun. I have, said he, often and often, in the course of the session, and the viccissitudes of my hopes and fears as to its issue, looked at that behind

the President, without being able to tell whether it was rising or setting; but now at length, I have the happiness to know, that it is a rising, and not a setting sun." ("Signing of the Constitution," by Thomas Prichard Rossiter, c. 1872/Courtesy, Independence National Historical Park)

Benjamin Franklin, at eighty-one the oldest delegate by far, was a crucial presence in reconciling conflicting views and reminding participants of the momentousness of the occasion: "I agree to this Constitution with all its faults, if they are such....It...astonishes me, sir, to find this system approaching so near to perfection as it does; and I think it will astonish our enemies, who are waiting with confidence to hear that our councils are confounded, like those of the builders of Babel....Thus I consent, sir, to this Constitution, because I expect no better, and because I am not sure, that it is not the best." (Portrait by Charles Willson Peale/Courtesy, The Pennsylvania Academy of the Fine Arts, Joseph and Sarah Harrison Collection)

Order of Procession,

In honor of the eſtabliſhment of the CONSTITUTION of the United States.

To parade preciſely at Eight o'Clock in the Morning, of FRIDAY, the 4th of JULY, 1788, proceeding along Third-ſtreet to Callowhill-ſtreet; thence to Fourth-ſtreet; down Fourth-ſtreet to Market-ſtreet; thence to the Grounds in Front of Buſh-hill.

I.
AN Officer, with twelve Axe-men, in frocks and caps.

II.
The City Troop of Light-Horſe, commanded by Colonel Miles.

III.
INDEPENDENCE.
John Nixon, Eſq; on horſeback, bearing the ſtaff and cap of Liberty.—The words, " 4th July, 1776," in gold letters, pendant from the ſtaff.

IV.
Four Pieces of Artillery, with a detachment from the Train, commanded by Captains Morrell and Fiſher.

V.
ALLIANCE WITH FRANCE.
Thomas Fitzſimons, Eſq; on horſeback, bearing a flag, white ground, having three fleurs-de-lys and thirteen ſtars in union, over the words " 6th February, 1778," in gold letters.

VI.
Corps of Light-Infantry, commanded by Capt. Claypole, from the 1ſt regiment.

VII.
DEFINITIVE TREATY OF PEACE.
George Clymer, Eſq; on horſeback, carrying a ſtaff, adorned with olive and laurel, the words " 3d September, 1783," in gold letters, pendant from the ſtaff.

VIII.
Col. John Shee, on horſeback, carrying a flag, blue field, with a laurel and an olive wreath over the words— " WASHINGTON, THE FRIEND OF HIS COUNTRY"—in ſilver letters—the ſtaff adorned with olive and laurel.

IX.
The City Troop of Light Dragoons, commanded by Major W. Jackſon.

X.
Richard Bache, Eſq; on horſeback, as a Herald, attended by a trumpet, proclaiming a New Æra—the words " New Æra," in gold letters, pendant from the Herald's ſtaff, and the following lines,
Peace o'er our land her olive wand extends,
And nabits roll'd innocence from Heaven deſcends;
The crimes and frauds of Anarchy ſhall fail,
Returning Juſtice lifts again her ſcale.

XI.
The Hon. Peter Muhlenberg, Eſq; Vice-Preſident of Pennſylvania, on horſeback, carrying a flag, blue field, emblazoned—the words " 17th September, 1787," in ſilver letters, on the flag.

XII.
Band of Muſic.

XIII.
The Honorable Chief-Juſtice M'Kean, The Hon. Judge Atlee, The Hon. Judge Ruſh, (in the Robes of Office)
In an ornamented Car, drawn by ſix horſes, bearing the CONSTITUTION, framed, fixed on a ſtaff, crowned with the Cap of Liberty—the words " THE PEOPLE," in gold letters, on the ſtaff, immediately under the Conſtitution.

XIV.
Corps of Light-Infantry, commanded by Capt. Heyſham, from the 2d regiment.

XV.
Ten Gentlemen, repreſenting the States that have adopted the Federal Conſtitution, viz.
1. Daniel Ingraham, Eſq;   New-Hampſhire.
2. Jonathan Williams, jun. Eſq;   Maſſachuſetts.
3. Jared Ingerſoll, Eſq;   Connecticut.
4. Hon. Chief Juſtice Brearley,   New-Jerſey.
5. James Wilſon, Eſq;   Pennſylvania.
6. Col. Thomas Robinſon,   Delaware.
7. Hon. J. E. Howard, Eſq;   Maryland.
8. Col. Febiger,   Virginia.
9. W. Ward Burrows, Eſq;   South-Carolina.
10. George Meade, Eſq;   Georgia.
Bearing diſtinguiſhing flags and walking arm in arm, emblematic of Union.

XVI.
Colonel William Williams, in armour, on horſeback.

XVII.
The Montgomery county Troop of Light-Horſe, commanded by James Morris, Eſquire.

XVIII.
An ornamented Car, drawn by four horſes, bearing Captain Thomas Bell, carrying the Flag of The United States,—Monſieur Barbe de Marbois, Flag of France,—Mr. Hunnicke, Flag of The United Netherlands,—Mr. Holſtead, Flag of Sweden,—Mr. Lucke, Flag of Pruſſia,—Thomas Barclay, Eſquire, Flag of Morocco,—States in alliance with America.

XIX.
The Judge, Regiſter, Marſhal, and other Officers of the Court of Admiralty, with their inſignia.

XX.
Wardens of the Port, and Tonnage Officers.

XXI.
Collector of the Cuſtoms, and Naval Officer.

XXII.
The Surveyor-General, Receiver-General, Secretary, and other Officers of the Land Office.

XXIII.
Regiſter, Recorder of Deeds, and Comptroller-General.

XXIV.
Peter Boynton, Eſq; and Colonel Iſaac Melcher, as an American and an Indian, ſmoking the Calumet of Peace, in a carriage drawn by two horſes.

XXV.
GRAND FEDERAL EDIFICE, on a carriage drawn by ten horſes, containing Meſſrs. Henry Baker, George Latimer, John Wharton, John Nixon, Samuel Morris, John Brown, Enoch Franciſcus, Joſeph Anthony, John Chaloner and Peter Graves, citizens of the Union.——
Attended by the Houſe-carpenters.

XXVI.
Corps of Light Infantry, commanded by Captain Rigs, 3th regiment.

XXVII.
The Agricultural Society, headed by their Preſident, S. Powel, Eſq;

XXVIII.
The Farmers, headed by Richard Peters, Richard Willing, Samuel Meredith, Iſaac Warner, George Gray, William Pollos, —— Barckbout and Charles Willing, with ploughs, &c.

XXIX.
The Manufacturing Society, with the ſpinning and carding machines, looms, &c. headed by Robert Hare, Eſq;

Corps of Light Infantry, commanded by Capt. Robeſon, from the 6th regiment.

The Marine Society, with their inſignia.

XXX.
The Federal Ship, The UNION, commanded by John Green, Eſq; Captain E. Smith, W. Belcher and Mr. Mercer, Lieutenants, with a proper crew of Officers and Seamen.

The Pilots of the Port, with a Pilot Boat.

Boat Builders, with a Barge.

The Ship-carpenters, Sail-makers, Rope-makers, Block-makers and Riggers.

The Merchants and Traders of the city and liberties of Philadelphia, headed by Thomas Willing, Eſq; with their inſignia—followed by the Merchants Clerks.

Corps of Light Infantry, commanded by Capt. Spear, from the 4th regiment.

TRADES and PROFESSIONS.

XXX.
1. Cordwainers.

XXXI.
2. Couch painters.

XXXII.
3. Cabinet and Chair-makers.

XXXIII.
4. Brick-makers.

XXXIV.
5. Painters.

XXXV.
6. Porters.

XXXVI.
7. Watch-makers.

XXXVII.
8. Fringe and Ribband Weavers.

XXXVIII.
9. Bricklayers.

XXXIX.
10. Taylors.

XL.
11. Inſtrument-makers, Turners and Windſor Chair-makers.

XLI.
12. Carvers and Gilders.

XLII.
13. Coopers.

XLIII.
14. Plane-makers.

XLIV.
15. Whip Manufacturers.

XLV.
16. Black-ſmiths, White-ſmiths, Nail-ſmiths and Bell-hangers.

XLVI.
17. Couch-makers.

XLVII.
18. Potters.

XLVIII.
19. Hatters.

XLIX.
20. Wheel-wrights.

L.
21. Tin-plate Workers.

LI.
22. Skinners, Breeches-makers and Glovers.

LII.
23. Tallow-chandlers.

LIII.
24. Butchers.

LIV.
25. Printers, Stationers and Book-binders.

LV.
26. Saddlers.

LVI.
27. Stone-cutters.

LVII.
28. Bakers.

LVIII.
29. Gun-ſmiths.

LIX.
30. Copper-ſmiths.

LX.
31. Gold-ſmiths, Silver-ſmiths and Jewellers.

LXI.
32. Diſtillers.

LXII.
33. Tobacconiſts.

LXIII.
34. Braſs-founders.

LXIV.
35. Stocking Manufacturers.

LXV.
36. Curriers.

LXVI.
37. Druggiſts.

LXVII.
38. Upholſterers.

LXVIII.
39. Sugar-refiners.

LXIX.
40. Brewers.

LXX.
41. Peruke-makers and Barbers.

LXXI.
42. Ship-chandlers.

LXXII.
43. Engravers.

LXXIII.
44. Plaiſterers.

Corps of Light Infantry, commanded by Capt. Rees, from the 2d regiment.

The Civil and Military Officers of Congreſs in the City.

His Excellency the PRESIDENT, and the SUPREME EXECUTIVE COUNCIL.

The Juſtices of the Common Pleas and the Magiſtrates.

Sheriff and Coroner, on horſeback.

City Wardens.

Conſtables and Watchmen.

The gentlemen of the Bar, headed by the Honorable Edward Shippen, Eſquire, Preſident of the Common Pleas, and William Bradford, Eſquire, Attorney-General, followed by the ſtudents of Law.

The Clergy of the different denominations.

The College of Phyſicians, headed by their Preſident, Dr. Redman.

Students of the Univerſity, headed by the Vice Provoſt, and of other Schools, headed by their reſpective Principals, Profeſſors, Maſters and Tutors.

The County Troop of Light Horſe, commanded by Major W. Macpherſon, bringing up the rear of the whole.

Major Fullerton to attend the right wing—Colonel Meaſe the left wing.

On the UNION GREEN, at Buſh-hill, Mr. WILSON will deliver an Oration, ſuited to the day; after which a Collation will be prepared for the company.

The following gentlemen, diſtinguiſhed by a white feather in the hat, are Superintendants of the proceſſion, General Mifflin, General Stewart, Colonel Procter, Colonel Gurney, Major Moore, Major Lennox, Mr. Peter Brown, Colonel Will, Colonel Marſh.

To add to the entertainments of the day, ten veſſels will be prepared and paraded as follows, one repreſenting New-Hampſhire, oppoſite the Northeaſt liberties,—the next for Maſſachuſetts, oppoſite Vine-ſtreet,—Connecticut, oppoſite Race-ſtreet,—New-Jerſey, Arch—Pennſylvania, Market—Delaware, Cheſnut—Maryland, Walnut—Virginia, Spruce—South-Carolina, Pine—and Georgia, south-ſtreet. The RISING SUN, under the command of Captain Philip Brown, will be anchored off Market ſtreet, and ſuperbly dreſſed. At night the will be handsomely illuminated.

By Order of the Committee of Arrangement,

Francis Hopkinſon, Chairman.

Philadelphia: Printed by HALL and SELLERS.

1787

"Tis done; we have become a nation."—Benjamin Rush

Original illustration by Warren Chappell
Art direction by Jessica Weber